D/5711

G000167844

LIVING AND DYING

The ultimate horizon?

Chris Wright

LION EDUCATIONAL
Oxford · Batavia · Sydney

Published by
Lion Publishing plc
Sandy Lane West, Oxford, England
ISBN 0 7459 2078 0
Albatross Books Pty Ltd
PO Box 320, Sutherland, NSW 2232, Australia
ISBN 0 7324 0498 3

First edition 1991

Acknowledgments
The author wishes to thank Sue Haines, co-author of the
Matters of Life and Death series, for her help with this book.

Design
Simon Jenkins

Quotations
We are grateful to those who have agreed to speak for their
faith; they cannot of course represent all views held by
adherents to the faith concerned.

We are also grateful to publishers and copyright holders for
permission to reproduce copyright material. The sources are as
follows:
Pages 3–4: adapted from a talk by Neil Elliott (set of discourses
from Madhyamaka Centre, Kilnwick, Percy Hall,
Pocklington)
Page 7: Anthony de Mello, *One Minute Wisdom*, Doubleday
Page 9: R. and V. Zorza, *A Way to Die*, Andre Deutsch Ltd
Pages 10 and 14: Debra Jarvis, *HIV Positive*, Lion Publishing
Page 11: Rabbi Harold Kushner, *Who Needs God?*, Simon and
Schuster
Page 12: W. Purcell, *A Time to Die*, Mowbrays
Pages 13 and 17: Stephen Levine, *Who Dies?*, Gateway Books
Pages 15, 16, 25, 29, 32: David Watson, *Fear No Evil*, Hodder
and Stoughton Limited
Page 21: Cicely Saunders, *Beyond All Pain* (now titled *Beyond
the Horizon: A Search for Meaning in Suffering*), Darton,
Longman and Todd
Pages 22 and 30: *The Koran*, tr. N. J. Dawood, Penguin
Books Ltd
Page 23: Professor John Bowker, *Worlds of Faith*, quoted by
permission of BBC Enterprises Ltd
Page 24: C. S. Lewis, *The Last Battle*, HarperCollins
Publishers
Page 26: John P. Hogan, *Here and There*, (publisher not traced)
Page 27: C. S. Lewis, *The Great Divorce*, HarperCollins
Publishers
Page 28: Michael Green, *What is Christianity?*, Lion
Publishing
Page 30: C. S. Lewis, *The Weight of Glory*, HarperCollins
Publishers
Page 31: R. Kendrick, *Examining Religions: Islam*,
Heinemann; Mary Batchelor, *Catherine Bramwell-Booth*,
Lion Publishing

All Bible quotations are from the Good News Bible, copyright
1966, 1971 and 1976 American Bible Society, published by
The Bible Societies and Collins except page 24, New
International Version, and page 25 (margin), Revised
Standard Version. All are reproduced by permission of the
copyright holders.

A catalogue record for this book is available
from the British Library

Printed in Malta

CONTENTS

THE INOPERABLE DISEASE

*T*oday approximately 200,000 people died. Some died by mischance, others by murder. Some by alcohol, others from starvation. Some died whilst still in the womb. Others of old age. Some died in peace with the world, others fighting all the way.

Death is the one certainty of life. But is death the end? Does the essential 'me' survive the disintegration of my body? How does belief in a life beyond death affect life here-and-now? Can it teach us not only how to die well, but how to live well?

I do not find it easy to accept that I am suffering from an incurable disease. Long before it was diagnosed – and my illness is terminal, irreversible, absolute – I had half-recognized it, since it runs in my family. I should have been expecting it. But it is only very recently that the seriousness of my disease has begun to sink in.

The condition from which I am suffering goes by the name of Mortality (the fact that I am born to die!) – that is what I have inherited from my parents.

One of the most sinister things of modern life is that we try to hide death – it takes place behind hospital curtains, 'out of sight; out of mind'. It is made mysterious, eerie. And yet it is the only thing of which we can be certain... it is the only thing which we can reliably predict will happen to us... we are all slowly, and sometimes not so slowly, turning into corpses. And yet for many death is a dirty word, not to be mentioned. What is it like? Why do we keep so quiet about it? What are we afraid of? Why the hushed silence?

The attitude many of us have towards our mortality has been illustrated by one speaker in the following way:

> **Supposing you're using the Edinburgh train through to London. You get on the train and think: 'This is very nice; I think I'll stay here for ever!' You put your name over the carriage; put curtains up in your compartment and think, 'Quite a nice little home'.**

Then you get to Edinburgh and the porter comes on and tells you to get off. But you're kind of clinging to the seat saying, 'I don't want to get off, this compartment's so nice.' The porter then tells you that it's in the nature of trains that you get off them at the end of the line. In reply you cry out, 'But I refuse to accept that.'

There's got to be some mature way of dealing with this; a painless way of getting off a train! But how do you do that? Well, the easiest way is to acknowledge when you get on the train that you've got to get off again, and not to get too comfortable.

It's the same thing when you find yourself inhabiting your body, your life situation: from the very beginning, acknowledge that you've got to get off again at some point. While I'm here, for sure, I can enjoy this carriage, this body; but I must not cling too tightly, because one day I will have to give it up. ❞

This illustration describes our tendency to cling desperately to things. The painless way of getting off the train is, of course, to accept the fact that you will have to get off when you start the journey – don't cling. Think for a minute:

➡ What are you aiming at in life?

➡ What is your attitude towards the world and people in it?

➡ Is there that secret desire to acquire – position, money, power, even to acquire people?

So often we live our life somehow ignoring the fact that one day we shall have to leave it behind. We spend so much effort grasping onto things that we make it hard to let go. And often we depart from this world suffering a death we cannot accept.

It was a truly human tombstone which bore the inscription: 'I expected this, but not yet'.

It is this lack of preparation, this being caught unawares, that makes the exit from the world so painful for some of us.

THINKING IT THROUGH

➡ What do you think of the train journey analogy? Does it correctly describe our attitude to death?

➡ Make a list of everything you own, everything you prefer, everything you want, everything you think of as 'you'.

That list is the gauge for measuring your possible resistance to death: these are the places where you are likely to cling!

➡ Why is it that we tend to cling to life?

➡ Do you think it is possible to 'enjoy this carriage' (ie enjoy living) without clinging onto life itself? Can you enjoy something without becoming absorbed in it?

➡ Why are we apparently unable to learn from the 'little deaths' (the various losses we suffer) along the way towards death itself?

A LIVING NIGHTMARE

What would it be like if you didn't have to die?

Is everlasting life a possibility? Is it desirable?

As far back as you can trace human history, people have engaged on a quest for the secret of everlasting life – if not in a physical sense at least by immortalizing their memory. The eighteenth-century philosopher Jeremy Bentham is wheeled out in his coffin at an annual Trustees' meeting to be present at its proceedings. The wife of the late President Marcos holds a birthday party for him every year, where people bring him presents.

In the scientific world of the twentieth century the quest for everlasting life has taken a new turn. The stories of Garret Smyth and Dr Martinot highlight this renewed interest.

THE DREAM OF IMMORTALITY

The Crionics Society offers people with a great deal of faith and money the opportunity to return from the dead. Its main base is in California, although recently a UK outlet has been established in Eastbourne, a town that is home for many elderly people. People in America have paid this society large sums of money to be frozen after death and stored at minus 196 degrees in the hope that science will discover some way to defrost them at some point far into the future. One such person is Garret Smyth, a British neuro-science student. He explains:

> **My head will be frozen when I die. At minus 196 degrees, any chemical changes would take millions of years. Almost everything will be curable in time. It's feasible that they may be able to replace organs with something artificial. If I'm old and my organs are knackered, why should I bother taking those with me? I value my life and see death as an adversary. I'm frightened of it as you would be of a conquerable enemy. I don't see any conflict between religion and crionics (the science of freezing bodies). If God exists, he's infinite and if I live for 1,000 years that's a blink of the eye for him. On the other hand, if he doesn't exist, I would be foolish not to be forever.**

The Independent on Sunday, 13 May 1990

THE CHILLING SECRET OF
DR MARTINOT

In 1984, when his wife Monique died from an ovarian cyst, Dr Raymond Martinot, a retired professor of medicine, put her in the deep freeze in the cellar of his French château. She has remained there since that day at a temperature of minus 55 degrees. Dr Martinot had originally built the deep freeze for himself, not at all expecting his younger wife to die before him.

Although no scientist at present thinks that there is a strong chance of bringing her back to life, he is willing to take the risk. As he says:

> 2050, or even 2100, what does it matter? It's a bet...with history. Double or quits. Monique has a 50-50 chance. If we lose, then she will have been deprived of much of her life, and we'll have been deprived of her.'

As a Catholic, he believes that Monique's body is in limbo. He wants the same for himself – there is room in the freezer for him when he dies.

> 'And meanwhile, at least we've been talking about Monique and bringing her back a bit... I am creating, like an artist.

Dr Martinot talks of Monique's death as her 'disappearance'; of the freezer as an 'engine' and of 'my hibernation business'.

Explaining what he has done, he says:

> I've always hated death and been afraid of it. Putrefaction revolts me. I did some research in the Institut de Froid in Paris, that's a commercial organization concerned with freezing foodstuffs, and that's when the idea hit me, in 1968 or so. If you can preserve food, why not bodies? I wanted my body to be preserved until science was capable of reviving it.

But, if we had it, what would life everlasting be like? In his book *Gulliver's Travels* Swift speculates on this question. He creates a land – the land of the Luggnaggians – in which, once or twice in a generation, someone is born who will never die. They are marked at birth by a circular red spot on their forehead. At first Gulliver thinks these children are the most fortunate imaginable, being born exempt from that universal calamity of human nature. However, as he comes to know them, he soon realizes how miserable and pitiable they are. As they grow old, their friends die around them, they become wracked with illnesses which have no release; their prosperity is handed on to their children and they look forward to an existence from which there is no escape.

THINKING IT THROUGH

➡ Both Garret Smyth and Dr Martinot admit that they are afraid of death. For Garret, death is his adversary. Which is the really frightening thing: death itself, the thought of dying, or the prospect of ceasing to exist?

➡ Look again at the words of Dr Martinot, who is frightened of depriving his wife of 'much of her life'. Is quantity of life important enough to be purchased at the cost of quality?

➡ There is a story of a teacher who was about to die. His disciples became depressed.

'Don't you see that death gives loveliness to life?' said the teacher.

'No. We'd much rather you never died,' said one disciple.

'Whatever is truly alive must die,' said the teacher. 'Look at the flowers; only plastic flowers never die.'

Adapted from *One Minute Wisdom*, by Anthony de Mello

Compare the teacher's view of death with that of a Garret Smyth or Dr Martinot. Which is the more realistic and/or the healthiest view?

➡ Is everlasting life a desirable hope?

DEATH: AN INVALUABLE HORIZON

> When a man knows he is to be hanged in a fortnight it concentrates his mind wonderfully.

Dr Johnson

We all know we are going to die some time, but cancer makes people face up to it... They are going to go on living with a lot of extra enjoyment, just because they have faced the fear of death. Cancer patients aren't dying. They're living. I have never seen a suicide because of cancer.

A New Zealand director of Radiology and Radiotherapy

There is a paradox to death. On the one hand it can be seen as a dreadful necessity (in the face of over-population, etc), and on the other as a valuable aid in learning to live well. The certainty of our death can add impetus to our living, bringing new power and seriousness to our life. It can wake us up, as Dr Johnson correctly said, to the importance of living – not just cruising aimlessly through life, achieving little, giving little.

In this chapter we look at how death can provide an invaluable horizon to our life, spurring us on to live wisely, fully. The two extracts which follow tell the stories of people who have been diagnosed as having cancer.

Robert Wilkins is a Quaker. He was told he had cancer less than a year before he wrote this letter. In this extract, he reflects on the lessons he has learned in the last twelve months.

At present the growths on my liver are contained and apparently inactive. Meanwhile, life has taken on a new vividness and sense of urgency. It is a most remarkable experience to be given notice of one's possible demise. One ensures that time is put to the fullest possible use. There is a new sense of priorities. Relationships are fully valued, and extremely rewarding. There is no time for the superficial. Interaction is at its most meaningful. I really want to know how this friend is faring, what problems and satisfactions he or she is encountering. The quality of life is indeed enhanced. Each day is used to greatest advantage, as *carpe diem* – seize the day – has become my motto. There is so much going on, I really have little time to be a patient.

Taken from *Oxford Friends Meeting Newsletter*, October 1990

THE VELVET AND THE ROSE

A Way To Die tells the story of a young teacher called Jane, who at the age of 25 learnt that she had cancer. Five months later, she died. It is a very moving story – the story of her journey through anger and bitterness at having to die so young, to a full appreciation of the life she still had left. A week before she died she asked for two everyday things as she lay in the hospice. One of these was a piece of velvet.

66 **It had been some time since Jane had asked for anything other than painkillers, cigarettes or an occasional sip of apple juice. There seemed to be nothing she felt a need for. But some memory must have stirred, for she asked, her words soft and slow: 'There is one thing… I suppose it's impossible…' The voice came as if she were speaking through a muffling curtain. 'You know how I've always loved velvet? I would like to touch velvet again before I die. I don't suppose it would be possible?'**

… in a short time there were three pieces of velvet for her to choose from. She smiled with pleasure as Dorothy gave them to her to touch, one by one. She chose the softest, a small oblong of deep pink silk velvet. Dorothy laid it on her shoulder so that she could feel its warm texture against her skin, and there it remained for the rest of her life…

Sue now brought a fresh rosebud from her garden. She laid it on the pillow beside Jane. Sue carefully pushed the stem of the flower into her hair, behind the ear, making sure that there were no thorns to catch her skin. From that time on, Jane wore a rose in her hair. When the first bloom withered, it was replaced. If the nurses had to turn Jane to keep her circulation going, or to give her an injection or make her comfortable, they always replaced the rose. The piece of velvet and the rose were handled with the greatest gentleness and delicacy, as if nothing in the world was more precious…

That afternoon Jane told Dorothy and Julia that she was happier than she'd ever been. 'The world is such a beautiful place. I know that now, I never really saw it before. I think I'm so lucky to be here, in the best place in such a lovely world.' She told them there was nothing more important in life than being born and dying. 'At birth,' she said, 'I knew nothing. At death, I know everything that I will ever know, and everything around me is good, not evil. That's a good way to die.' **99**

Before her illness, Jane had taken so many things for granted – everyday things, like the rose and the piece of velvet. Now these everyday things came to have added importance. We are all like this – we take so many things for granted, often until it is too late.

A Way To Die, The story of Jane Zorza, by R. and V. Zorza

Some people dying from AIDS have experienced a creative re-ordering of their lives – a change in perspective. A number of AIDS patients speak of their experience in the small book *HIV Positive*, by Debra Jarvis.

66 AIDS has made me see that the most important things in my life are my relationships with others. That gives me a lot of joy, but also a lot of pain, since some of my relationships are broken. 99

66 Not being an athletic person, I always hated that slogan, 'No pain, no gain'. I spent most of my life avoiding any kind of pain. AIDS has made me get to know pain in a new way. Some of the medicine I was on at first made me feel sicker than ever. At that point I learned that when I tensed up, or tried to distract myself, my pain actually seemed worse. It is paradoxical, but the more I just allowed myself to be in the pain, look it right in the eye, the less intense it became. I can't explain how this works – I can only tell you that it does.

Because of being with the pain, I have seen sides of myself that I had never seen before. Sides that I like! Sides that I admire! I wish I could have seen these sides some other way – I don't recommend going out and contracting AIDS so you can find yourself. Anyway, I hate to admit it, but now I understand and agree with 'No pain, no gain'. 99

66 I don't expect to be cured. Now that doesn't mean I don't *want* to be cured or *hope* to be cured. I am always hoping that there is some miracle drug right around the corner. But now I feel like this: it's OK to die of AIDS and it's OK to be cured of AIDS.

Don't get me wrong: I am not thrilled I have AIDS. But I realize that some things have happened within me that could not have happened if I had been physically well. I mean things like a healing of my spirit, an acceptance of myself, an opening to God. So in a way I am healed even when my T-cells are down. I would not trade this feeling for anything in the world. 99

In the view of all the writers quoted, death is not the enemy at all. Instead, it adds significance and importance to our life. It may, after all, be our friend, 'our sister death', as St Francis called it.

On the sundials of some old monasteries are the words *memento mori* ('remember that you have to die'). And there are some on which has been written *memento viveri* ('remember that you have to live') – and there is really no difference between the two.

The Rule of St Benedict challenges monks to incorporate the awareness of death into every moment of their daily life, so as to become more fully alive. In this way death rather than terminating life can contribute to it. However, this is only possible once we see death, not in isolation, but in relation to other parts of life – fitting into the pattern.

In the next chapter we explore what it means to live in preparation for death.

➡ 'It is not death that people find frightening; it is "the shadow of death", the knowledge, which no other animal lives with, that one day we will die.'

H. Kushner, *Who Needs God?*

Do you think this is true? If so, why?

➡ What would it mean for you to live by the motto *carpe diem* ('seize the day')?

➡ Jane chose a piece of velvet and a rosebud as two very ordinary things which she treasured. What would your choice be?

➡ What do you think 'to live wisely' means?

LEARNING TO DIE

You may be thinking, 'Isn't all this rather morbid; why on earth spend time thinking about the moment of our death now, when we could be out there enjoying ourselves and really living?' Others will say, 'I'll cross that bridge when I come to it.'

We have already suggested that death shocks us: it has a tendency to creep up on us from behind when we are least expecting it. But, treated as part of life, it can add seriousness and meaning to what we do.

Some people have gone even further, suggesting that it is dangerous to deny death. A more healthy attitude is to prepare for it. This chapter considers why it is important to prepare for death, and explores ways of doing it.

Think for a moment: Tomorrow could be the first day of twenty-five years of multiple sclerosis. How would you react? What inner resources do you have to cope? How could you develop those inner resources, so that you are able to face whatever may happen in life?

Many people live their life without giving a thought to their end, half hoping they will be able to cross that bridge when they come to it. But how realistic is this attitude? When pain could be wracking your body, tiredness seeping through every pore, how realistic is it to think that you will be in a fit state then to prepare for your death? Imagine trying to work out a difficult mathematical equation with two huge hi-fi speakers blasting rock music down your ears. Extreme pain and fear of death can be as disturbing as that.

The need to prepare for death in the midst of the experiences of life is often highlighted by people who work closely with the dying and bereaved. As one medical social worker said, 'If you live in a mess you are likely to die in one.' Timothy West, Medical Director of St Christopher's Hospice, says:

> **Faith or courage do not often make their first appearance at the deathbed. However, if such virtues have at least been recognised during a... lifetime it is often at the time of dying that their reality and strength are revealed. All our lives we are preparing for death.**

Quoted in W. Purcell, *A Time to Die*

None of this is new. In the seventeenth century a number of religious writers pointed out the importance of using the experiences of life as a preparation for death. Bishop Jeremy Taylor wrote two volumes entitled *Holy Living* and *Holy Dying*. They are tightly linked together for, as he writes: 'be ready for (death) by the preparations of a good life'.

READY FOR ANYTHING

I can't die yet.

I haven't said goodbye.

I'm not ready, I'm scared.

I haven't tidied up my business.

A person who works closely with dying people wrote:

Few participate in their life so fully that death is not a threat... Most fight death as they fought life.

Stephen Levine,
Who Dies?

The list of reasons could be endless, because for many death interrupts life, like an unwelcome visitor at a party. More than that, it brings life to a stop, and exposes the party for what it really was. The prospect of death fills people with dread as a host of uncertainties and doubts arise in their minds. 'I'm not ready, I'm not ready, I'm not ready.'

So how can we get ready? The following extracts offer some suggestions.

Death is the one thing over which we have no control. This is why it is so frightening. When it suddenly appears on the horizon we are confronted by something we have not planned and often cannot handle.

Most people spend their lives pursuing pleasure and avoiding pain, as though pain were the great enemy. So they try to hide feelings of insecurity, fear and doubt, half-pretending that they don't exist. Instead of facing up to these unwanted feelings they bury them deep within. The feelings are not worked through and do not go away. They stay there deep down inside, waiting to raise their ugly head – grasping the moments when we are most vulnerable, least in control.

This is why so many people are unprepared for death when it comes – they first have to deal with a morass of hidden emotion. Dying well becomes an almost impossible task.

A patient dying of the AIDS virus talks of this submerged mass of feelings which he had to deal with as the prospect of death reared its head:

Two small boys saw their grandmother walking up and down reading her prayer book. One boy said to the other, 'What's Grandma doing?' The other boy replied, 'She's swotting for her finals!'

> It seems bizarre – now that I know I have AIDS, I actually feel more whole than I ever did before. I am sure it is because I have asked the Light into my life, and I have been forced to face death. For me that meant looking at areas of my life that I have always put on hold.
>
> Now I just don't have that much time to waste. Death is not frightening to me since I feel that I have made peace with myself. In fact, I think that death is not the end of the journey. It is like going to Kansas City on your way to somewhere else. Kansas City is no big deal; it's the rest of the journey that's important. Unfortunately, no one has come back from death (as they have from Kansas City) to tell us what it is like. So we make a big deal out of it.

Quoted in Debra Jarvis, *HIV Positive*

Pain, as Debra Jarvis puts it, 'can be like a sharp knife. It slices through years of pretension, hiding and fakery to reveal our true selves. Selves that we kept from unfolding. Selves that we need to love and accept. Seen in this way, pain can indeed give birth to a new being.'

GIVE AND TAKE

In ordinary life we use scores of idioms that speak of taking – we take a bath, a walk, a trip; we take an exam or a course. It is therefore not surprising that after a life in which we firmly take charge we find it so difficult in the end to handle something which we cannot control: death takes us.

The secret lies in learning to give and let go – to give ourselves. What we take for granted does not make us happy. What we hold onto deteriorates in our grasp. What we take offence at we make into a hurdle we can't get past.

But in giving thanks, self-giving, giving up and forgiving we die a little here and now and paradoxically we become more fully alive. We also become ready for the final death.

➡ What do you think the AIDS patient meant by 'making peace with myself'?

What are the things that make this difficult in your own life?

➡ How could you become 'more fully alive'?

➡ Would you like to know, have warning, when you are going to die? Would you live life any differently if you knew?

THIS IS THE MOMENT

*E*ach of us, whatever our age, is old enough to die. So how can we put this knowledge to good effect in our lives?

QUALITY OR QUANTITY?

We have seen that some people cling so desperately to life that they will go to any lengths to extend it. Even more are shocked by the way death creeps up on us when we are least prepared for it.

People who work closely with the dying see the tragic words 'If only...' written on many faces: 'If only I could have done this' or 'If only I hadn't done that' – as if death had robbed them of the time to live a complete, fulfilled life.

But is the long life the complete one? Or does the quality of a person's life depend upon other factors?

David Watson was a vicar in the Church of England. On 5 January 1983 he discovered that he had cancer. A year later he died. In that year he wrote a book called *Fear No Evil* in which he speaks with honesty of his year-long struggle.

> **'What if you are not healed?'** I am sometimes asked. Although it does not help to dwell on that question too much, I realise that it is a perfectly fair one... Of course I cannot know that I shall have ten to twenty years more to live. I cannot know that I have even one. But that is also true of every one of us. With all our planning for the future, we need to live a day at a time and enjoy each day as a gift from God. 'This is the day which the Lord has made; let us rejoice and be glad in it' (Psalm 118:24). Some Christians speak of the sacrament of the present moment: we need to live not just a day at a time, but moment by moment...

Like David Watson, people who work closely with the dying often come away from these encounters feeling that what is important is the NOW – not the past or the future, but the present. As Jane Zorza discovered, there is a call to live each moment to the full, to appreciate what the 'now' has to offer, not taking anything for granted. When we answer that call we find that quality of life does not depend upon how long it lasts but upon how deeply it is lived.

LIVING 'IN THE LIGHT OF ETERNITY'

For the Christian the present moment is precious because it offers an opportunity to live fully in relationship with Jesus. The length of time is not important in itself – what is important is the quality of life. Thus Christians use the term 'eternal life' to mean not life that goes on for ever in time (a nightmarish prospect for many!) but life lived in relationship to Jesus – beginning here and now and continuing beyond the earthly barrier of death. As David Watson puts it:

> 'Eternal life', said Jesus when praying, 'means knowing you, the only true God, and knowing Jesus Christ whom you sent' (John 17:3). Nothing is more important than our relationship with God, both for this life and for the next.
>
> A doctor complained recently, 'Our patients expect us to make them immortal!' Many cling tenaciously to this life because they fear there is nothing more to come. Today's preoccupation with youth and youthfulness demonstrates the same deep-seated anxiety about the future, especially that last enemy death, of which cancer seems the most frightening symbol.
>
> One day we stand to lose everything of this world, and no one knows when that day will come. Once we have lost our lives to God, however, we belong eternally to him; and in Christ we have all that is ultimately important… God offers no promise to shield us from the evil of this fallen world. There is no immunity guaranteed from sickness, pain, sorrow or death. What he does pledge is his never-failing presence for those who have found him in Christ. Nothing can destroy that. Always he is with us. And, in the long run, that is all we need to know.

THINKING IT THROUGH

➡ If how we die is linked to how we live, what should our lives be like to ensure that we 'die well'?

➡ One response to mortality is to live fully in the present. What do you think this means in everyday life?

➡ Imagine you are lying in an emergency room, critically ill, unable to speak or move. You vaguely see the faces of loved ones hovering around your bed. You want to reach out to them, to tell them something, to finish your business with them, to say goodbye.

– Look at your relationships, one by one. How much would you have to work out before you were ready to say goodbye? What might 'unfinished business' mean to you in this situation?

– Do you think it is inevitable that people will always die with unfinished business in hand?

WHO DIES?

How would you describe yourself? A good worker...A sporty sort of person...Likes heavy metal music...The list could be endless. But notice how often people identify themselves with what they do, or what they like. What happens, then, when these things are taken away through prolonged illness or death? Who are you then?

> Imagine that you are lying in bed, with your new car parked in the drive, realising that you may never again drive that car of which you were once so proud. Your shoes are sitting by the closet; you know you may never wear them again. Your children are playing in the next room, but you are too weak to get up and join them. Your mate is cooking supper in the kitchen for the children and another meal for you, which she will have to spoon-feed you because you are too weak to feed yourself. Your digestive system is no longer able to withstand the food you so much enjoyed in the past. You want to get up and help, as you always have, but it is no longer possible. Indeed, you sense that in a year from now your mate may well be making love to another and that, in a short time, someone else might be raising your children. Looking over at your closet, you see hanging there the clothes you so enjoyed, clothes you sense you will never wear again and which someday may be worn by someone you've never met. And you ask yourself, 'Who was that stylish person who bought those clothes?' Because it's not you any more. All the motivation for buying these clothes, and adorning the body, seems so confusing as the body dwindles, losing twenty, thirty, forty, fifty pounds or more. Who was it that went out and bought those clothes?
>
> You're watching your body get weaker and weaker. You can't take care of the children. You can't make love. You can't earn a living. You can't even go to the bathroom by yourself. Who are you now?

Stephen Levine, *Who Dies?*

Some people become so identified with what they do (their job, their role in the family) that they become incredibly insecure at the time of death, when all of these things are being threatened.

Just for a moment, try making a list of what you are – greedy, moody, kind, helpful... Then ask yourself:

➡ does the picture hold together, or are there contradictions/ opposites? For example, if you are both kind and greedy, which is the real you?

➡ does this list fully describe who you are? Is it an exhaustive list, or are bits missing?

➡ does this list capture the *real* you, or does it miss something? If so, what is it that is missing?

In Buddhist thinking there is no 'self' which forms the core of our personality. We are not the sum of our emotions (because these change from minute to minute, day to day, depending on circumstances). Therefore we cannot say that *we are moody*, for example. Furthermore, Buddhists point out that since there is nothing permanent within us, there is nothing within ourselves we can be identified with.

They like to use different images to illustrate this point, comparing the self to a candle flame, a water jet, a wave, a ripple...

THE CANDLE FLAME

Imagine a row of candles. One candle passes on its flame to the next before it burns out.

➡ Is the flame of the candle that is going out the same as the flame of the candle being lit?

➡ What do all the candle flames have in common and how do they differ?

➡ Take any flame: is the flame burning at evening watch the same flame still burning at morning watch? What is the same? What has changed?

Buddhists understand that just as the candle flame changes and yet remains constant at the same time, so also the self is a changing thing. Buddhists use this image of the row of candles to illustrate the flowing nature of the self.

THE WAVE

The water in the wave which we see rapidly approaching on the seashore never arrives at our feet. It is the shape of the wave which arrives. A wave is obviously not a chunk of water moving across the sea's surface. It is the water moving up and down.

So Buddhists understand the self, not as a 'chunk' which does not move but as something fluid.

I have met people who, when approaching death, say that

they have never lived so fully. They become awake to who they are – no longer identifying with certain emotions, or roles, nor dreaming of who they may become. So often people live their lives in a prison made of models and ideas of how things are or should be, must be, will be: hoping for the future, regretting the past and in the meantime forgetting to live in the present, robbing the 'now' of its importance. Death, as we have already discovered, can be seen as a horizon which makes us refocus on life in the present.

The following Buddhist meditation explores what this might mean:

ACCEPTING DEATH
A Meditation

So now try, without self-deception, fully to accept the fact that 'I am going to die'. It is as if I were in the condemned cell. There will come a time when my body will exist no more, and there is nothing I can do to avoid it. This body will totally disintegrate. Moment by moment my life is ticking away, always getting shorter.

Most of the things I value in this life – the people around me, my friends and relatives, my children and my lover, all of my possessions and my wealth – even my body – I will have to leave behind and depart alone. The most important thing now is for me to use this life to follow a spiritual path.

To use this life to indulge in trivial worldly pursuits, when I must encounter death at the end of it, is a great waste. So my spiritual practice must be very pure – just going through the motions is not enough. I must actually practice.

THINKING IT THROUGH

➡ If you were asked, 'Who are you?', how would you reply?

➡ How do you respond to the Buddhist idea of no-self? Can you list anything which is permanent about you?

➡ How do you respond to the sentiments expressed in the Buddhist meditation? Do you think it is a great waste to spend this life without thoughts of following a spiritual path?

➡ It is often said that people relate to each other in very selfish ways. People use others for what they can get out of them. How might this Buddhist idea of having no permanent self change your relationships?

LIFE AFTER DEATH

*I*s there life after death? Most of the world's major faiths believe in some form of life after death. In this chapter we consider some of these beliefs. But first we look at this general belief in an afterlife. The extracts which follow explore this hope.

> Death is nothing at all...
>
> I have only slipped away into the next room... I am I, and you are you... whatever we were to each other, that we are still. Call me by my old familiar name, speak to me in the easy way which you always used. Put no difference into your tone; wear no forced air of solemnity or sorrow. Laugh as we always laughed at the little jokes we enjoyed together. Play, smile, think of me, pray for me. Let my name be ever the household word that it always was. Let it be spoken without effort, without the ghost of a shadow on it. Life means all that it ever meant. It is the same as it ever was; there is absolutely unbroken continuity. What is this death but a negligible accident? Why should I be out of mind because I am out of sight? I am but waiting for you for an interval, somewhere very near, just around the corner. All is well.

Henry Scott Holland

> I am standing on the sea shore. A ship sails and spreads her white sails to the morning breeze and starts for the ocean. She is an object of beauty and I stand watching her till at last she fades on the horizon and someone at my side says, 'She is gone.' Gone where? Gone from my sight, that is all; she is just as large in the masts, hull and spars as she was when I saw her, and just as able to bear her load of living freight to its destination.
>
> The diminished size and total loss of sight is in me, not in her; and just at the moment when someone at my side says, 'She is gone', there are others who are watching her coming, and other voices take up a glad shout, 'There she comes', and that is Dying.

Source unknown

IN THE MIDST OF LIFE

Death and I are only nodding acquaintances
We have not been formally introduced
But many times I have noticed
The final encounter
Here in this hospice,
I can truly say
That death has been met with dignity
Who can diving the thoughts
Of a man in close confrontation?
I can only remember
One particular passing
When a man,
With sustained smile
Pointed out what was for him
Evidently a great light
Who knows what final revelations
Are received in the last hours?
Lord, grant me a star in the East
As well as a smouldering sunset.

Cicely Saunders, *Beyond All Pain*

I have seen death too often to believe in death. It is not an ending, but a withdrawal. As one who finishes a long journey Stills the motor, turns off the lights, Steps from the car And walks up the path to the home that awaits him.

An American poet, in *Beyond All Pain*

AKHIRAH – LIFE AFTER DEATH – IN ISLAM

One of the basic Muslim beliefs is that of *Akhirah* – life after death. Life after death is described in a physical way in the Qur'an, and for this reason Muslims do not cremate their dead, but instead bury their bodies as soon as possible after death before they begin to decay. Muslims believe that these bodies will be raised to life again on the Day of Judgment.

For those who die before the Day of Judgment the souls are taken to *barzakh* (a state of waiting) by the angel of death, Azrail.

On the Day of Judgment all souls will be rewarded or punished, depending on how they have lived this life. The reward for the righteous will be heaven. This is vividly described in the Qur'an:

❝ You shall enter gardens watered by running streams in which you shall abide forever... A wall with a gate shall be set before them. Inside there shall be mercy, and out, to the fore, the scourge of Hell. (The righteous) shall recline on jewelled couches face to face, and there shall wait on them immortal youths with bowls and ewers and a cup of purest wine (that will neither pain their heads nor take away their reason); with fruits of their own choice and flesh of fowls that they relish... Those on the right hand – happy shall be those on the right hand! They shall recline on couches raised on high in the shade of thornless sidrahs and clusters of talh; amidst gushing waters and abundant fruits, unforbidden, never ending.

Suras 57;56

Hell (*jahannam*) is the reward for unbelievers. It too is described in vivid language:

As for those on the left hand (wretched shall be those on the left hand!) they shall dwell amidst scorching winds and seething water: in the shade of pitch-black smoke, neither cool nor refreshing. For they have lived in comfort and persisted in the heinous sin, saying: 'When we are once dead and turned to dust and bones, shall we, with all our forefathers, be raised to life?'

Say: 'This present generation, as well as the generations that passed before it, shall be brought together on an appointed day. As for you sinners who deny the truth you shall drink boiling water yet you shall drink it as the thirsty camel drinks.'

Such shall be their fare on the Day of Reckoning.

Surah 56

THE HINDU BELIEF IN REINCARNATION

For the Hindu, death is not the end but merely the separation of the soul from the body. The body dies and the soul carries on its eternal journey. Hindus believe in reincarnation: that the soul is re-embodied according to the law of *karma*. This is a moral or behaviour law which states that a person's present condition is determined by how he/she has lived in their previous existence. Consequently the individual is wholly responsible for his/her present condition and future.

Hindu tradition suggests that the last stage in a person's earthly existence should be one spent in preparation for death. At this stage in life all family responsibilities have been carried out and a person can concentrate on spiritual matters.

Hindus cremate their dead, since they believe that this releases the soul for its continued journey.

A young Hindu wife explains how this belief in the law of *karma* affects how she lives her everyday life:

'*Karma* encourages me: when I think that we are going to come back, then I want to do good things, and I want to do my prayers so that God doesn't punish me. He won't punish me if I do good things. I'm always scared if I do anything bad; if I lie, or if I do anything wrong to my husband, if I do anything wrong to my mother-in-law, then God might punish me for doing wrong things. So I always have these things in my mind when I do something wrong. I always go to that photograph of Ram, and do apologise; I say, "Please forgive me for that and guide me." I think God is there, and he's always watching us, what we are doing, wrong or right. Every time I start doing something wrong, I always get an instinct that I am doing wrong – I shouldn't do this. It's always God who stops me doing that. I'm not scared of my husband or of anyone else. Whenever somebody stops me, it's always God. I feel that thing in my mind, that God is watching me, and if I'm doing anything wrong, he will definitely punish me. When I die, he'll punish me.'

That may sound like religion born of fear. But in fact it is closer to justice – that our deeds *will* get their reward.

J. Bowker, *Worlds of Faith*

THINKING IT THROUGH

➡ Do you think that belief in life after death is a strength or a weakness?

➡ Cremation versus burial! Does it make a difference?

➡ Is belief in *karma* merely a rule by fear or a just explanation of the inequalities in the world?

BEYOND ALL PAIN

Malcolm Muggeridge's words sum up the Christian's belief that death is not the end to be feared but an opening into a greater life with God. This chapter explores what this life will be like.

THE CHRISTIAN HOPE

Before Jesus died he promised his disciples that he was going to prepare a place for them:

> **Do not let your hearts be troubled. Trust in God; trust also in me. In my Father's house are many rooms; if it were not so, I would have told you. I am going there to prepare a place for you. And if I go and prepare a place for you, I will come back and take you to be with me that you also may be where I am.**

John 14:1-3

In his children's story, *The Last Battle*, C.S. Lewis echoes the excitement of the homesick schoolchild in his picture of life beyond the grave:

> **Then Aslan turned to them and said, 'You do not yet look so happy as I mean you to be.' Lucy said, 'We're so afraid of being sent away, Aslan. And you have sent us back into our own world so often.' 'No fear of that,' said Aslan. 'Have you not guessed?'**

Their hearts leaped and a wild hope rose within them. 'There *was* a real railway accident,' said Aslan softly. 'Your father and mother and all of you are – as you used to call it in the Shadowlands – dead. The term is over: the holidays have begun. The dream is ended: this is the morning.'

And as He spoke He no longer looked to them like a lion; but the things that began to happen after that were so great and beautiful that I cannot write them. And for us this is the end of all the stories, and we can most truly say that they all lived happily ever after. But for them it was only the beginning of the real story. All their life in this world and all their adventures in Narnia had only been the cover and the title page: now at last they were beginning

The expectant thrill of life beyond the grave is captured in the words of Ben Travers (who died in 1985, aged 95). In his autobiography he said that he did not expect or desire a tombstone, but that, if he did have one, he would like engraved on it these words:

This is where the real fun begins.

This sentiment sums up the great hope which was offered by Jesus.

Chapter One of the Great Story which no one on earth has read: which goes on forever: in which every chapter is better than the one before.

The Christian hope of the resurrection is based firmly on Christ's resurrection:

The worst times for me were at two or three o'clock in the morning. I had told countless thousands of people that I was not afraid of death since through Christ I had already received God's gift of eternal life. For years I had not doubted these truths at all. But now the most fundamental questions were nagging away insistently, especially in those long hours of the night. If I was soon on my way to heaven, how real was heaven? Was it anything more than a beautiful idea? What honestly would happen when I died? Did God himself really exist after all? How could I be sure? Indeed, how could I be certain of anything apart from cancer and death? I literally sweated over those questions, and on many occasions woke up with my pyjamas bathed in cold sweat! Never before had my faith been so ferociously attacked...

I was as convinced as I possibly could be that Christ had risen from the dead, and this was the solid ground for my own future hopes. Death is not the end. There is life after death. Death is only putting out the lamp at the rise of a new dawn.

I am not saying that I never had any problems after that. It would not be true. But in the middle of those nightmare storms, with waves of doubt and fear lashing all around me, I found that my faith was secure on that immovable rock of Christ.

David Watson, *Fear No Evil*

If Christ has not been raised from death, we have nothing to preach and you have nothing to believe... But the truth is that Christ has been raised from death, as the guarantee that those who sleep in death will also be raised... For just as all people die because of their union with Adam, in the same way all will be raised to life because of their union with Christ.

1 Corinthians 15:14,20-22

Christians believe that eternal life is a gift from the generous God who has set them free from sin and death.

Christians use words like 'transformation' when they attempt to speak of this resurrection life. The resurrection of the body suggests a richness of life – the old body transformed and fully alive in the new heaven and the new earth. This is the description given in the last book of the Bible, Revelation chapter 21:

> Then I saw a new heaven and a new earth. The first heaven and the first earth disappeared and the sea vanished. And I saw the Holy City, the new Jerusalem, coming down out of heaven from God, prepared and ready, like a bride dressed to meet her husband. I heard a loud voice speaking from the throne: 'Now God's home is with mankind! He will live with them, and they shall be his people. God himself will be with them, and he will be their God. He will wipe away all tears from their eyes. There will be no more death, no more grief or crying or pain. The old things have disappeared.'

WHAT HAPPENS AFTER DEATH?

Within the teaching of Jesus there is reference to judgment, when all will be called to account for their lives. There will be a separation between those who love God and enjoy his presence in heaven and those who have chosen otherwise. The concept of separation (heaven and hell) is a difficult one, which the following story may help us to understand.

A KOREAN LEGEND

In Korea there is a legend about a native warrior who died and went to heaven. 'Before I enter,' he said to the gatekeeper, 'I would like you to take me on a tour of hell.' The gatekeeper found a guide to take the warrior to hell. When he got there he was astonished to see a great table piled high with the choicest foods. But the people in hell were starving. The warrior turned to his guide and raised his eyebrows.

'It's this way,' the guide explained. 'Everybody who comes here is given a pair of chopsticks five feet long, and is required to hold them at the end to eat. But you just can't eat with chopsticks five feet long if you hold them at the end. Look at them. They miss their mouths every time, see?'

The visitor agreed that this was hell indeed and asked to be taken back to heaven post-haste. In heaven, to his surprise, he saw a similar room, with a similar table laden with very choice foods. But the people were happy: they looked radiantly happy.

The visitor turned to the guide. 'No chopsticks, I suppose?' he asked. 'Oh yes,' said the guide, 'they have the same chopsticks, the same length, and they must be held at the end just as in hell. But you see, these people have learned that if a man feeds his neighbour, his neighbour will feed him also.'

John P. Hogan, *Here and There*

The following picture attempts to describe that without God's help we would all be judged unfit for the life of heaven. However, it also stresses the positive gift of life which God offers to all:

We can liken judgment to arriving at a party. I ring the doorbell of this very smart house – the owner's son has personally invited me. The door opens. I stand nervously awaiting the questions which the doorman will surely ask of me to justify my presence. But they never come because at that moment the son, my friend, appears. He greets me warmly, and leads me into the warmth and brightness inside, saying to the doorman over his shoulder – 'It's all right, she's with me.' I have been accepted not because of who I am but because of who he is, and he has invited me.

Thus the Christian concept of judgment is not primarily about condemnation. Christians believe in a God who offers salvation to all who wish to take it. There is a cost, and that is to accept God as the sovereign of your life. What this will mean in practice is to allow God to rule in your life – your thoughts, motivations and actions. And thus the idea of judgment is connected with that of self-judgment. If you've never really examined yourself in this life – judged your thoughts, your feelings, motivations and actions – you will not be ready to face the final judgment. The concept of judgment can be viewed as an encouragement to live a fulfilled life, one which will include self-awareness and self-judgment.

Jesus taught that people bring judgment upon themselves:

'This is how the judgment works: the light has come into the world, but people love the darkness rather than the light.'

John 3:19

Christians believe Jesus' promise to his followers:

'I give them eternal life, and they shall never die. No one can snatch them away from me.'

John 10:28

They can be certain of this. But they are also accountable to God for the way they live and this has a huge impact upon their lives. The biblical image, as we have already seen, is not so much of an almighty God with the scales of justice, but of self-choice.

In his book *The Great Divorce* C.S. Lewis illustrates Jesus' teaching by showing that the innumerable choices we make in life inevitably determine what follows.

There are only two kinds of people in the end: those who say to God, 'Thy will be done', and those to whom God says, in the end, 'Thy will be done'.

TRANSFORMATION

What will the resurrection life be like? What will we be like? The Bible teaches that instead of a physical body which is subject to pain and sickness, weariness and decay, God gives us a spiritual or resurrection body.

When St Paul describes what this spiritual or resurrection body will be like he points his readers to an analogy from nature:

When you sow a seed in the ground, it does not sprout to life unless it dies. And what you sow is a bare seed, perhaps a grain of wheat or some other grain, not the full-bodied plant that will later grow up.

1 Corinthians 15:36-37

There is little if any resemblance between the seed and the beautiful flower which rises from it, and so...

This is how it will be when the dead are raised to life. When the body is buried, it is mortal; when raised, it will be immortal. When buried, it is ugly and weak; when raised, it will be beautiful and strong. When buried, it is a physical body; when raised, it will be a spiritual body.

1 Corinthians 15:42-44

By the help of the analogy from nature Paul illustrates two things: the resurrection body will be utterly unlike the present body. Yet there is a continuity, as between seed and plant.

A NEW DIMENSION

The Swallowtail caterpillar is not a particularly beautiful beast. Not very mobile. Only interested in eating...
But the caterpillar comes to a stage when its caterpillar life must end. It grows uninterested in eating. It becomes restless. It spins itself a cocoon, and turns into a chrysalis. To all intents and purposes it is dead. But really it is very far from dead. That caterpillar existence is transformed into the totally new dimension of living enjoyed by the butterfly. And the Swallowtail butterfly is extremely beautiful. It is highly mobile. It is interested in flowers and sunshine. It soars high among the trees.

So it is with Christians after death. Here on earth we are not very beautiful creatures, despite the grace of God at work in us. Often we are selfish, earthbound in our interests. There is something restless about us.

But when we die, that is not the end of us. We emerge into the sunshine of God's home – the same people we were on earth, only wonderfully transformed. The caterpillar has turned into a full butterfly. No longer selfish. No longer earthbound. But free to enjoy the totally new dimension of existence beyond the grace.

Michael Green, *What is Christianity?*

THINKING IT THROUGH

➡ Why do you think C.S. Lewis called this earthly life 'Shadowlands' in comparison with the afterlife? Do you agree with this description?

➡ Why do you think that many feel the concept of hell to be a difficult one? Is that of heaven easier?

➡ Do you think that the concept of judgment is a useful one in helping people to lead fulfilled lives?

➡ Should life be accountable, or is the idea of judgment just a crude threat?

P.S.

❝ In one sense, the Christian is not preparing for death. Essentially he is preparing for *life*, abundant life in all its fullness. The world, with its fleeting pleasures, is not the final reality, with heaven as a shadowy and suspect unknown. The best and purest joys on earth are only a shadow of the reality that God has prepared for us in Christ... when the body of the Christian dies, the really wonderful journey has only just begun. ❞

David Watson, *Fear No Evil*

❝ For this reason we never become discouraged. Even though our physical being is gradually decaying, yet our spiritual being is renewed day after day. And this small and temporary trouble we suffer will bring us a tremendous and eternal glory, much greater than the trouble. For we fix our attention, not on things that are seen, but on things that are unseen. What can be seen lasts only for a time, but what cannot be seen lasts for ever. ❞

2 Corinthians 4:16-18

LIVING WITH IMMORTALS

*I*n this chapter we bring together ideas found elsewhere in the book on how belief in an afterlife affects the way people live in this life.

C.S. Lewis felt that belief in the afterlife necessarily affects how you relate to other people:

> **There are no *ordinary* people. All people are potential immortals... this awareness cannot help but affect how we live with them on earth.**
>
> **It is in the light of this possibility that we should conduct all our dealings with one another, all friendships, all loves, all play, all politics. It is immortals whom we joke with, work with, marry, snub and exploit.**
>
> **This does not mean that we are always to be serious. We must play. But our merriment must be of that kind which exists between people who have, from the outset, taken each other seriously – no flippancy, no superiority. And our love must be real.**

C.S. Lewis, *Weight of Glory*

For the Muslim, belief in life after death has a great bearing upon the way life is lived on earth, since Muslims believe that they will be accountable after death:

> **Each soul is the hostage of its own deeds. Those on the right hand will in their gardens ask the sinners: 'What brought you into Hell?' They will reply: 'We never prayed or fed the hungry. We engaged in vain disputes and denied the Day of Reckoning till death at last overtook us.'**

Surah 74.40-47

> Every soul shall be paid back according to its deeds, for Allah knows of all their actions.
>
> Qur'an, Surah 39.70

This accountability after death creates in the Muslim a sense of God-consciousness (called *taqwa*):

> **Being in a state of *taqwa* is quite different from ordinary living. It alters Muslims' entire motivation for doing things, and stops them doing many things that would**

give a great deal of selfish pleasure. Being aware of the 'eyes of God' alters even the way they think.

R. Kendrick, *Examining Religions: Islam*

Thus for the Muslim all people are responsible for their own life after death. They consider that this life on earth is a test of our characters, and the way we react to life determines our future life.

(The significant difference between this account of judgment and the way a Christian sees judgment is that Christians believe they will not be punished for the wrong they have done, because Jesus took that punishment on their behalf when he was crucified.)

> At evening, do not expect to live till morning, at morning, do not expect to live till evening. Take from your health for your illness, and from your life for your death.

Hadith, quoted in Kendrick

TOO HEAVENLY-MINDED?

Does belief in an afterlife make you want to leave this earthly existence? In her biography of Catherine Bramwell-Booth, granddaughter of the founder of the Salvation Army, Mary Batchelor recounts a conversation between Catherine and Malcolm Muggeridge:

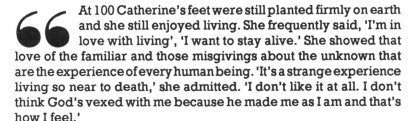

At 100 Catherine's feet were still planted firmly on earth and she still enjoyed living. She frequently said, 'I'm in love with living', 'I want to stay alive.' She showed that love of the familiar and those misgivings about the unknown that are the experience of every human being. 'It's a strange experience living so near to death,' she admitted. 'I don't like it at all. I don't think God's vexed with me because he made me as I am and that's how I feel.'

Malcolm Muggeridge spent a day at North Court in conversation with Catherine for a television programme to mark her centenary.

'I got a dressing down from her,' he said, 'because I said that I was looking forward to departing and she wouldn't have that at any price. She said that was a ridiculous thing to do, that life was good and wonderful and she herself hoped that although she was now 100 she would continue. She was pulling my leg a little, I think.' She was probably not, because a few years earlier, when Peter France had asked if she agreed that death, as well as life, might be a thrilling experience, she replied:

'Oh no, I think death is awful.'

There is good reason for Catherine's feeling. The Bible itself describes death as the last enemy – the enemy God will destroy when he makes all things new.

Others witness to the fact that belief in a life with Christ beyond death helps them through the pain in this present. This is the testimony of David Watson as he lay dying from cancer:

> When all the false promise of the world is stripped away like old wallpaper (or at least threatened), the only solid reality that matters before God is that Christ has died for us to bear all our sin, and has been raised from the dead, giving us a living hope in the face of our last enemy...
>
> You know, actually to be with Christ and free for ever from the pain and suffering, tears and all the problems and injustices of this world, there is nothing more glorious than that. That is why I genuinely am at the place where I really want to be in heaven (sometimes the sooner the better), but I am willing to be on this earth, with all its struggles and battles if he wants me here.

He echoes the words of St Paul from his prison cell:

> What is life? To me, it is Christ. Death, then, will bring more... I want very much to leave this life and be with Christ, which is a far better thing; but for your sake it is much more important that I stay alive.

Philippians 1:21,23-24

THINKING IT THROUGH

➡ 'There are no ordinary people. All are potential immortals.' In what ways could this view enable people to treat each other, and life itself, more seriously, more preciously?

➡ Would this life be poorer without a belief in the afterlife, or does such a belief not make any practical difference?

➡ Compare the feelings of Catherine Bramwell-Booth and Malcolm Muggeridge. Whom do you feel closest to? Why?

We shall rest and we shall see,
We shall see and we shall love,
We shall love and we shall pray,
in the end which is no end!
For what is our end but to reach
that Kingdom which has no end?

St Augustine, *City of God*